MW01089937

ALL THE BIRDS AWAKE

ALL THE BIRDS AWAKE

BY GAYLE KAUNE

TEBOT BACH • HUNTINGTON BEACH • CALIFORNIA • 2011

© 2011 by Gayle Kaune. All rights reserved. No part of this book may be used or reproduced in any manner whatsoever without written permission except in the case of brief quotations embodied in critical articles and reviews. For information, address Tebot Bach Permissions Department, Box 7887, Huntington Beach, CA   92615-7887 USA.

Cover painting: Martha Pfanschmidt
Design, layout: Melanie Matheson, Rolling Rhino Communications

ISBN 13:   978-1-893670-77-8
ISBN 10:   1-893670-77-5

Library of Congress Control Number: 2011931961

A Tebot Bach book

Tebot Bach, Welsh for little teapot, is A Nonprofit Public Benefit Corporation which sponsors workshops, forums, lectures, and publications. Tebot Bach books are distributed by Tebot Bach, Small Press Distribution, and Armadillo.

The Tebot Bach Mission: Advancing Literacy, Strengthening Community, and Transforming life Experiences with the power of poetry through readings, workshops, and publications.

This book is made possible in part by a grant from The San Diego Foundation Steven R. and Lera B. Smith Fund at the recommendation of Lera Smith.

www.tebotbach.org

ACKNOWLEDGMENTS

The author gratefully thanks the following places where these poems first appeared.

Fishdance: "The Explorer Dreams of Sacajawea" under the title "In the Sound Between Notes"
Greenfield Review: "Writers' Club"
Northwind Anthology 2005: "The Wife Speaks to Her Husband"
Northwind Anthology 2006: "In These Canyons"
Northwind Arts Association website: "Red Shrine under Madrona Tree"
N-Sid-Sen Star from Thimbleberry Press: "The First Night," "The Last Morning"
Passages North: "Michigan Autumn"
Poets Against the War website: "Anna Maria Island"
Pontoon: "When It Happened"
A Shimmering Field from Writer's Haven Press: "The Middle-Aged Woman Rearranges Her Life"
The Smoking Poet: "There Is This Thing About Blood," "Three Girls and a Pony"
Thirty First Bird Review: "Souvenir"
Weathered Pages from Blue Begonia Press: " Clusters of Starry White Flowers"
Whitefish Review: "Hanford Reach"
Some of these poems appeared in an earlier chapbook, *Concentric Circles,* winner of the Flume Press Award from Flume Press.

I want to thank everyone who has made this book possible. Starting with the Rattlesnake Mountain Writers—Dan Clark, Georganne O'Connor, Dixie Partridge, Rita Mazur, Jim Thielman, and Bill Wilkins—with whom I spent many desert evenings developing my craft. And, after moving across the mountains, to the Madrona Writers, past and present—Tom Aslin, Dianne Butler, Teri Cholene, Janet Cox, Michael Hanner, Toni Hanner, Jenifer Lawrence, Ellie Mathews, Bob McFarlane, Bonnie Nelson, Don Roberts, Karen Seashore, Diana Taylor, David Thornbrugh, Richard Widerkehr, and Carl Youngmann—with whom I spent amazing residencies during which many of these poems were inspired. Thanks to the Centrum Foundation for their support of those residencies. Special thanks to Jenifer Lawrence, who read an earlier version of this manuscript, and to

Richard Widerkehr, who met tirelessly with me through ferry cancellations and coffee shop remodels as we went over poems. I am especially indebted to my husband, Bill, who has provided enduring support and a physicist's sense of order to my life, both creative and otherwise. And finally, to Mifanwy Kaiser and Tebot Bach for bringing this book to the reader.

—for my family

CONTENTS

I

Hanford Reach 3
There Is This Thing about Blood 4
I'm Reading a Poem and There It Is Again, That Word *Capacious* ... 5
Instructions 7
Red Angels 8
Eureka Motel 9
Anna Maria Island 11
Souvenir 12
Three Girls and a Pony 13
Alaskan Cruise 14

II

Light and Dark Are Reversed on Film 19
Michigan Autumn 20
Take the Knife Away 21
Clusters of Starry White Flowers 23
White Ballet 24
Writers' Club 27
High School Biology Class 28
In the Gallery 29
The Explorer Dreams of Sacajawea 31
The Wife Speaks to Her Husband 32
The Middle-Aged Woman Rearranges Her Life 33
Our Woman Turns Over a New Leaf 34

III

This Constant Penance 39
Burning the Records 41
The Café Is a Chapel for Sunlight 42
Four Months after Surgery 44
About the Friend 45
The Friend Speaks 46
Red Shrine under Madrona Tree 47
Two Poems from Camp:
I. The First Night 48
II. The Last Morning 49

Bathing Cyrus   50
Vacation Maui   51
Still Awake at 2 AM, Quoting Whitman   53
Thai Bus Trip   54
After the Woman Left Orvieto   57
The Day the Plein Air Painting   58
The Buddha Says   59

IV
Magellan's Right Turn   63
Forgetting the Word for Weep   65
The Geri-Psych Ward   66
The Woman Could Not Forget   67
When It Happened   68
Also the Rising   69
Three Poems with Light   70

V
This Story, This Happiness   75
Where We Come From   76
Where Do They Go   78
The Stones and the Weather   79
All the Birds Awake   81
Ketchikan   82
Alchemy   84
Anniversary: Icicle Creek   86
How Were We to Know   87
Because at the Core   89
We're at a Summer Gathering—   90
In These Canyons   91
The Columbia: A Baptism, 1975-2005   93

I

Hanford Reach

This is the Hanford Reach, fifty-one miles of free-flowing river,
land preserved in its purity because of nuclear reactors.
                    —U.S. Government brochure

Sage sparrows, white pelicans,
Great Blue Heron in tree top rookeries. . .

It's all a prayer to the natural
world as if the sand cliffs
known as white bluffs
could erase the outline
of plutonium reactors,
as if the sky, clean and clear now,
could forget the toxic fumes
of the "green run" of forty-nine.

I have come here with my family
—husband, two grown daughters—
fifty miles upriver on a jet boat,
the roar of the motor silenced
as we drift along the cliffs.

It's 104 degrees and with the heat
peace descends on the river.

                    * * *

War is over, and Jimmy Gladwell
leaves recess early because he's crying.
I'm back in Vegas, 1955,
the morning an A-bomb
explodes in the desert
and the boys tell Jimmy he's a sissy
because he'd been afraid to get up and cheer.

I'd risen at five with my family,
huddled on the porch
in my white gown,
waited for the flash, the roar,
sunrise on the crimson cloud.

There is this thing about blood

the menstrual blood that doesn't stop
until we are drained,
anemic, transfused, transfixed,
like some pale saint
in Raphael's paintings but it's not art,
it's my daughter, my other daughter,
and myself, the years of clots
big as golf balls. It's one bruise
after another and how was I to know
it's passed on? And here we are, the bloody
noses of childhood and all the surgical
weeping. It's blood and we've all got a thing
about it, and last week when the hematologist
tells us it's so rare he's never seen three
generations of it passed down, transformed,
I want to snatch my newborn grandson
away from his needle, tell him, *That's enough!*
And when my daughter speaks of her hard, long labor—
no epidural because of possible paralysis,
I long to ask her to stop talking,
but I've got to listen, I'm the one who started this—
Storage Pool Disease—but it's okay I tell myself,
as I see the photo of the dark, red placenta
coiled on a steel tray, a spongy mass,
a thing some people eat,
something to remind me
this is not about loss, but life.

I'm reading a poem and there it is again, that word *capacious*

as if the poem were roomy
enough and wouldn't mind
if the poet put that big word inside
its granite bones. When my friend the biology
teacher calls, she tells me about the skeleton
her students named Napoleon Bonaparte.
On her desk is a purple dachshund
which occasionally disappears, ends up in the case
with "Nappy," propped against his pelvis in an obscene
yet funny way. She is advisor to the Anime Club
and the G-L-B-T "Tolerance" club—two groups of high
school kids that hang out in her room during lunchtime.

We laugh for an hour and when I hang up
I have to face the day, waiting for me like a Fabergé egg,
all decorated with appointments and "shoulds,"
though thank goodness I don't have to chop
twenty onions like yesterday when we served
chili to the men without homes.

The homeless surprised me. I expected
to see the rough, maybe mentally ill,
I see on the streets in the city, but last night,
in my small mill town, they were clean-cut
and young, nothing like the guy last week
whose picture was in the big city paper for stabbing
a woman on my daughter's street.

I exaggerate. It was eight blocks away
from her street, a good thing I ended up
in a church basement serving spinach
salad with cranberries or I'd be stuck
in a stereotype of fear. And when we went to the church
it was snowing, unusual for here—the coldest
day of the year, and why should I worry
about putting the word *capacious* in my poem,
or my life, as in years past when *paradigm*

kept showing up or *heuristic*, or that other one,
luminous, which could describe my earlier thoughts
as I tried to look each man in the eye,
hand him a cup filled with milk,
or last night's moon on the snow
as we walked to our cars,
carrying the scorched pots.

Instructions

When you return from war
don't arrive early evening,
your mother scraping carrots
at the sink, garbage disposal wailing.

Don't take a cab right up to the front
curb. "What's that taxi doing here?"
your sister calls from the kitchen
where she's writing a science paper.
Father, watching the news, replies,
"I don't know."

Nobody knows this skinny
man—*it couldn't be*—who steps out
of the car, turns to pay
the driver, (Now, we've gathered
at the window, his back is to us—
the brown and green
combat fatigues loose
on his frame, faded pants
tucked into ankle-high boots.)

When you return, call first.
Don't hop a military transport
weeks ahead of schedule,
then take a seventy-dollar
cab ride and rush home, nonstop,
to turn towards us and walk up the steps,
one by one,
your pale face
a stiff grin,
while we're yelling and crying,
"It's Glenn! It's Glenn!"

When you come home from war
don't arrive in a flag-draped
box. But showing up unannounced—
sometimes people can hardly bear
such happiness.

Red Angels

On my desk, a flyer
from the ballet *Red Angels*.
Two dancers: he bends forward,
she leans back, their red leotards
outlined by the darkness of an empty stage.

I am indoors this winter
afternoon waiting for dusk
and a repeat of yesterday's performance:
pink moon rising against a cardinal mountain.

I missed that moonrise last evening.
I was sitting here, in near darkness,
stunned, having hung up the phone—
a dear friend's brother-in-law murdered,
body not released because of brutal
stabbing. And just the day before
another friend's cancer had re-appeared,
magician-like, in her bones.

I write notes of sorrow on my only cards,
crimson O'Keefe poppies, then move
to the front room and sit on the wine-colored
couch, look at Mt. Baker guarding a lavender bay.

Tonight, if the mountain
appears washed in red,
I will be a witness.

Eureka Motel

Sleep well at the Eureka Motel
Eureka, Kansas. Heart of the United States.
Center of the Magic Circle.
                    —Eureka Motel postcard, Eureka, Kansas, 1955

After the seventh day,
after the heavens and earth and
    the sky.
After the mongoose and rose,
    the Tualatin River, the Pleiades
    Constellation, the Pilchuck Mountain.
The Everglades—that river of grass
    with its osprey and egrets,
Montepulciano and the hill towns of Umbria,
the North, East, South, and West banks of everything,
Patagonia and Tanzania,
Adam and Eve.
After all that and the seventh day
    of resting,
God created the magic circle—
a giant compass with His belly
at the center. Face down,
he stretched out, and spun in a ring,
and whatever his fingers encompassed,
that became his kingdom,
and everything within it was blessed
with tornadoes and hurricanes,
floods and flies and maggots,
mosquitoes bringing malaria,
bellies swollen with hunger,
malnutrition, dysentery,
the wars with their peasants arms flying,
nuclear wars with their threat of winter.
And while he was at it, he poked
some holes in the ozone.

And because it was a circle, it held
the firmament and contained all
polarities of sunlight and storm:
the Blessed Virgin offsprings

with their wide-eyed wonder. All
the beauty we come to call God
was also held in this realm.
Except at the center,
the eye of the needle,
the center of the Magic Circle
where sits the Eureka Motel
a u-shaped wonder with fifty-two
rooms for one hundred and four people
who can live here in harmony knowing
neither good nor evil.

                    Come,
you will be blessed with unremarkable
health, the air thoroughly conditioned,
your thoughts so comprehensible
no one needs to speak. Sex is unnecessary
(though the beds have magic fingers)
for, as we know, love brings both pain
and bliss. Cream of Wheat will be delivered
by twenty-four-hour room service
and the black-and-white television
will entertain you with stories
of real life.

Anna Maria Island

—for Anne and Bob, on the eve of the Iraq War

Today, on this blue-green gulf
I watch two egrets
whose fine white feathers, *aigrettes*,
wave in the breeze. Miles away
is the beginning of war.

One egret, tamed by a neighbor,
steps toward me—begging,
I suspect, though its beauty
is as pure as the bouquet
of white roses
—symbol of welcome—
left by our hosts
on the bedside table.
Or, did they choose white
for peace? In such small
gestures we state
our intentions to survive
on a planet that survives.

Each moment we refuse
to attack does not signal
retreat. It means we hold
the idea of one humanity
in our future—hand of God,
if you will—as these birds
who grace us now,
this tropical winter,
hold in their being
the long flight home.

Souvenir

—*The Expulsion of Adam and Eve,*
in Santa Maria del Carmine, Florence.

There is too much pain in this picture,
Adam and Eve leaving the Garden.
He holds his face in both hands.
She has one arm across her breasts,
the other hand hiding the place
between her legs—shame
and all that colors that feeling,
though they could not name it—
Masaccio painted this fresco
on the chapel wall, and I have
the postcard pinned to my wall—
parking lot outside.
And why, here, now—
the colors pale teal bleeding
into orange, and all that flesh—
Adam's ribs outlined, his genitals
exposed;
Eve, mouth open,
eyes covered in shadow.
She looks blind, but isn't.
They both see
how only in loss is shame
defined, whether it's yours
or someone else's.

Three girls and a pony

stand outside Angkor Wat.
The pony is dressed with a gold halter,
red saddle, blue strap behind his ears.
The girls, about twelve, have turned
their backs to the pony for a moment
and are huddled together
laughing, talking of boys.
Tourists walk by. Nobody
puts a child on the pony
for a photo because it is winter
in faraway places; all the children
are home and in school,
though not these girls,
here, in Cambodia.

Reflected in a wide pool is the temple—
once a place of prayer, homage
to the gods. Now, a mecca
for tourists from Korea, Japan,
the U.S. The pony knows nothing
of this; he worships the three girls,
their hands offering sweet treats,
their clear voices
always singing his praise.

Alaskan Cruise

It was a city unto itself
and sixteen hundred travelers lived
there hurling themselves out to sea.
There were the servers and the served.
The servers had brown skin, and the served, white.

In the brochure: balconies off your private
cabin, 24-hour service—stewards at every call—
(Brie, carnations, truffles!)
an endless supply of white towels
waiting to be tossed on the floor.

Not in the brochure: crew below decks
in dorms without windows,
less than minimum wage,
fourteen-hour days, six-day weeks,
fourteen-month tours
away from their families.

Naturally, the servers spoke the white ones'
language, with an accent, of course,
though we couldn't even pronounce their names.

The ship held us all, a large mother,
who wants her children to get along,
and we did: *Drink of the Day, Glacier Tonics,*
Blue Ice Margaritas—they spun their magic—
though the workers didn't drink.

How did they handle it, then?
Was it the water and stunning landscape—
mountains and glaciers—sliding past?
Or the silent animals, watching from shore?

Hardly. It was money;
and it came from our work, far easier—
sitting behind desks, gazing at computers,
speaking into phones.
How we brought it with us stuffed

everywhere: pockets, purses, even our mouths
and ears were filled with bills—tens and twenties,
the occasional hundred; it dripped from us
as we strolled on board and ashore.

We left it lying around like candy,
we threw it away like flyers.
And we signed our name and cabin number
everywhere (they brought us little slips of paper)—
our autograph! For a while,
we were gods.

II

Light and Dark Are Reversed on Film

As I click the camera,
today's wind ghosts the hair
of children, now grown,
gathered for reunion.

I turn to photograph
the past: empty swings
rock beside the blind tree
in an overexposed garden,
its statuary reminiscent of baby graves.

       * * *

It's all so real, these scenes of domesticity,
they must be photographed by family,
so intimate are the gestures.

In the background people busy
themselves with a violin or a meal.

But the pictures are taken by a poet,
whose only skill is words.
She doesn't realize how happiness
can destroy itself when placed
under glass—doesn't know to set
the meter, the mistake of too much light.

Michigan Autumn

Suppose it is Fall and you are five—
scuffing stiff leather shoes
along the sidewalk—kicking leaves.

You wear your red jacket, carry
a new pencil box. At school,
during "rest-time," you lie
on the braided rug, gaze
at the tops of trees as they slowly
scatter leaves.

You think of Mother, at home,
making Ovaltine; Father,
shoveling coal in the basement.
Maybe today Grandma Baker
will invite the neighborhood
kids for a bonfire.

You taste her limp raisin cookies,
flex sore fingers as they try to lever
the long-handled rake against
giant piles of leaves; perhaps
this year it will be easy.

You remember the fire, the smell
of autumn smoke while waiting
for Grandma to pass out lollipops.
You taste the translucent sweetness,
dream the flames in their Indian dance.

Take the Knife Away

and what do you have? Trying
to get through life without sharp
edges. Take the knife away
and the childhood was beautiful:
ten acres of meadow and woodland,
Goshorn Creek with its bounty of white balls
from the golf course upstream. The stable
was heaven—Blondie, Salty, Blaze
chewing oats, the closed air, the smell of straw.

            The horses chewing oats
while a young girl, nine, stands on a stool,
leans across the Dutch door, tells them stories.
She strokes their faces, watches their eyes
return a peaceful gaze.

A peaceful gaze is what she carried
from that time. There would be future freeways,
computers ticking obligations, sobbing patients,
sick children, police rushing to a stop beside
her wrecked cars.

Oh, maybe that peace was from Mother singing,
carrying laundry outside to the line
while Yukon, the husky, circled her feet.
Or maybe it came from her older brother
teaching her to catch gophers: put a glass jar
over their back door, pour water down their front door.

It's hard to tie it to one thing—
how they canned peaches
from the backyard tree. After the jars
were filled and capped, Mother let her screw
on the rings.

It's like that sometimes,
the horses in the stable,
the mother in the kitchen,
the child chasing monarchs

and painted ladies, the asparagus growing wild,
then going to seed, the sun drying out the fields
and irrigation pipes running water
from the creek: *psst, psst...*

I have almost forgotten how we dug holes—
booby traps—covered them with tarpaper and sand,
tried to lure Doug, from down the street,
to walk across one, fall into a hole.

         I could fall into a hole
trying to write about childhood:
the greenhouse across the street—
how we played chase up and down
the rows of chrysanthemums,
took hoses, had water fights
whenever Doug's father and mother
were out delivering flowers
for a wedding or a funeral.

Car crashes were best—
maybe 8, 10 cars piled up
on the icy highway (so many Services!
so many deliveries!) his parents would be busy
for days. Alone, we'd run the aisles
hiding and seeking—gray winter
outside, framed by the glass,
my own home holding its own kind of frieze.

But there, in the greenhouse, it was warm
and moist. There, among the hothouse
tomatoes and white baby's breath,
I breathed my way into a happy childhood,
careening across the concrete floors, dirty hoses
coiled everywhere, puddles of water
soaking my feet.

Clusters of Starry White Flowers

Cinderella had muscles—otherwise how could
she shovel the stones, bleach the hearth,
use an anvil for a chisel?
And when she snapped the stems of vines,
clipped the climbing peas, chopped
onions for soup, did she bury her rage
like women of the kitchen,
her words clotted
by the thimble of her sex?

A prince will always be nemesis,
taking courage away in a pumpkin coach,
placing his hands on the white pedestal
of her breasts when no one is looking.
And she, so charmed by this fiery hold,
bracelets her rescue by his touch, elbows
her way into the heart of old godmothers
who want to forget the young women who dreamed
of escape and were trampled by rising hooves.

White Ballet

Those. . . dancers. . . are part of a grand classical ballet tradition, the blanc, or white, ballet. Dating back to the 19th century, they feature an all-female white-clad corps de ballet, usually representing some otherworldly presence. . . such an assignment is a rite of passage for a dancer.
                    —Seattle Post-Intelligencer

Her life had started as a kind of ballet;
she a swan in flight, trying
to move with what was spoken,
choreographed, to become part of the corps,
yet live her own life.

Those were the days of cheap wine
and girdles; sex a game of baseball: bases,
hits and home runs—all rated plays—
the girl in charge of holding the rules. We lived
in Vegas then, cockroaches everywhere.

At night, they'd crawl up the tub drain.
If you went into the bathroom
and flipped on the light they'd scurry
away. If you stayed in the dark,
you could hear a whispering sound
their feet made, like a mantra,
be a good girl, be a good girl,
and I was. I ate the liver Mother fried
and once, when I was anemic—
hemorrhaging periods—I had to eat
it every day for weeks.

The church was a place on the corner
where my friend Kathy prayed.
I'd kneel with her after school,
pretend I knew the mumbled Latin,
longed to be absolved by the priest
for skinny-dipping in the neighbor's pool
while they were on vacation.

Away on vacation was what they said
about my family. We were always gone,
taking road trips, getting
out of school. I borrowed books
from the library, read my way
cross-country in the back of our
station wagons, trying to be part of
the family ballet, to remember
all the rules I had eaten
for breakfast, lunch, and dinner
in the two-bit cafes.

In truck stops men
would stand outside smoking.
I wondered if I could stow myself
in a rig, leave my family for one
of those truckers. Like the young
bride of Jerry Lee Lewis, could
I run away?

Oh, I didn't really want
to get away. I was thirteen;
my life was about to feather
into a fantasy: maybe this or that.
I still wore orange, pointy
shoes, clicked my heels
like Dorothy in the *Wizard of Oz,*
wondered who the wizard of my future
would be. We all did that,
spun 45's and lay on our beds,
listening to the words
that trapped us in the myth—
our music for the ballet—never aware
of the chiaroscuro of background noise,
the shadow of desire and cockroaches
painting its way into our dreams.

Later, there were car crashes
and drunken parties, Carol
stealing money so she could hire
a backdoor abortion, Jill always

ending up in jail, the police
not believing her story.

I listened. I took all this in
as if my life depended on the ability
to chew my past into some kind of future,
my need to take the best of this hit-and-miss
adolescence and dance my way into a new scene:
to pirouette out of that desert town,
leaving my white gloves and cotton panties
hanging on the farthest manzanita tree.

Writers' Club

We are sealed in the basement of a bank listening
to a story about a pickle that talks.
The room is muraled in autumn forest—four panels.
The friendly pickle is trapped in a quart jar,
his stump-like arms helpless against the glass.

I see only a fetus, floating in brine,
that our junior high teacher was rumored
to keep on a shelf in the back.

One night, after biology club,
Mr. Foscarini forced me to look;
made me promise never to tell.

That year our group sold
pink ceramic dachshunds with ballpoint
pens for tails. We took the profits
and chartered a bus to Disneyland which
back then wasn't even finished, Tomorrowland
still a vision, and the monkeys on the Amazon
not yet programmed to screech.

High School Biology Class

Ruby Harrington demanded silence
as we dissected frogs, poked ventricles
with military precision, took out the liver,
kidneys, unraveled the mystery of frog intestine,
then sketched it all in artist's ink.

I had a crush on a guy named Loveless, my dark-haired
partner in frog lab. But greasy-haired Mrs. Harrington
was without love, her voice hoarse from yelling,
her newlywed husband doing research in Antarctica,
an expert in some kind of freezing.

Fifteen frogs, thirty students, and each day for weeks
the teacher screaming, *Wayland!* at this wisecrack kid
and pelting him with blackboard erasers
from across the room.

We were used to Ruby's temper, so were surprised
one day in spring when she smiled, leaned back,
and called us "honey," her hair in a freshly washed bob,
her lips outlined in red that was her name.

And she didn't notice if Wayland goofed off during lab
—we were dissecting cats by then, three per class,
pulled from the freezer that morning, and all the girls
refused to cut, dropping their scalpels and screaming—
Wayland, as always, egging us on,

but Ruby didn't look up. She gazed in the mirror
and primped, the smell of formaldehyde a heady perfume;
husband flying home late that afternoon.

In the Gallery

Written in response to 20 different entries in an art show in which two separate paintings by women artists have the same title: *Winter Longing.*

The women in the paintings
are waiting
to find a new hat
to wear. They are waiting
for the leaves to turn orange and drop
into the water beside the festival boats.

They are waiting in black leotards,
turquoise bra straps revealed,
leaning into the floor gracefully.

They collect teapots made of clay,
ride bicycles nude, in the park.

Their hair falls out from chemo,
they gather at coffee for talk.

They imagine they are Thumbelina
and rock in a cradle suspended from the sky.

It doesn't stop their waiting.

They enter anonymous relationships
their fingers blue from touching icy hearts.
They tell the raven of passion,
"Not now." And wait.

How can so many women leave
the red chair of their life,
travel through a tiny doorway
shaped like a beehive?

How can they forget
the domestic animals of their home pasture,
or leave their city outlined in black and white
with its Times Square preacher,

cross the wide sands of a winter desert,
to hover like stuffed hummingbirds
over the ampersand of their fantasies
until their bodies glow with the jeweled
prophecy of Cassandra's secret and a man
comes by to unclasp their longing?

The Explorer Dreams of Sacajawea

soon he would be calling
her name her name the ghost
birds that fly south would speak
her name as they write his longing
across the shoulder of her blue
sky as river enters the heart
of her country it was all light
it seemed
and even shadow had a geometry
that was pleasing
love and birds
are what kept him going small flutterings
in the grassy space of his mind
large migrations in the path
of his heart oh it was true
sometimes he knew that like
water he was more in touch
with longing than arrival

The Wife Speaks to Her Husband

It could be done with praise
but instead she only tries to pause,
to brush away the shades
of melancholy and form clear red
words from lips stained
with kisses never sent, harsh
with restraint and longing,

and the need to stitch
two halves together,
the need to let nothing go to waste
as if this were a perfect world,
one in which a rose ordered is a rose
delivered, sitting outside on terra-cotta
steps in a crystal vase about to explode.

But it's really not that hard,
and harder. The roses are delivered
without water; their eyes
grow dry and crack, their mouths
curtained with the words a broken
angel might say: *Love is red*
but so are wounds, and which is wider?

I could reach out and spread my arms
as far as sky to bind you to me
and you still might leave.

The Middle-Aged Woman Rearranges Her Life

Summer, you're cleaning the last
drawers and find a basket of beads
you bought, years back, from a shop,
high in the Beartooth Mountains.
Little labels—*peridot, alexandrite*—mark
each glass. Remember the golden lab
that lounged in the corner and the small
mutt sleeping on the chair? It seemed easy,
then, stringing people and possibilities
along like these beads.

And what enters your mind now,
insistent as the crazy mower
you keep hearing down the street,
is there are so many kinds of strings—
tiger wire, memory wire, the sinew bobbins—
And you want to go back, to hike that river,
the Stillwater, but you know about grizzlies,
though your friend—all ninety-five pounds
of her—claimed she could carry
a gun; but what could have really
happened, two women alone with a bear?

And no, it's not a lawnmower; it's a chipper—
chewing up prunings and trimmings.
And you want to put everything
you ever clipped and pruned and hacked—
back together—like these porcupine claws, wolf claws, reproduction
eagle claws from the shop—all the talk
you interrupted, thinking you knew what the other
would say—all the relationships that did not move
forward. Maybe they were meant to remain suspended;
poised—the summit of the mountain,
the eye of the grizzly, these beads,
resting in a basket years later,
still unstrung.

Our Woman Turns Over a New Leaf

It's not easy, change—
first, close the door
on fear. Say you fall in love
with your garden all over again,
or you start to sew—a stitch
here, a ripped seam there.

Say, you design a website
for women considering plastic
surgery. Before: the dour face;
after: the same face,
but smiling—no surgery—

they've given the $4,000 for blepharoplasty
or the 6 for rhinoplasty or the 16k
(full lift!)—to a school
for orphans in Cambodia.

The women fly there, surround
themselves with radiant students—
their "after" face, aglow.
People ask, "What have you done?
New hair? New makeup?"
They reply, "New school.
Cambodia."

But we're talking about change,
the only predictable word
in the English language. Outside
my window, an old woman walks, bounces
really, in a youngster's body. She must
be coming from the yoga studio
down the street.

What would the yogi say
about change?
"Put it in the donation box."

What would the Buddhist monk
say? "I'll give you a blessing, wave
incense back and forth across your face
but I can not touch you, you are a woman.
My assistant will tie these strings
to your wrist, bring you luck."

Though luck is really about change,
isn't it? No one asks for luck
when everything is smooth;
it's the roller coaster careening
across the rotting pier that needs luck.

And myself? Give me that body
that stretches and moves
like a thirty-year-old's.
Here, cut these foolish strings;
I'm on my way.

III

This Constant Penance

The ancestors of happiness are hiding
in funeral pyres and caves.
I peek inside, ask guidance
for the journey: iodine and camphor
help, the smoking fires of paradox.

I believe in gray as middle ground
between black and titanium white.
This is the day men arrive in metal
cylinders, pulled from deep in the earth.
This is the day the ghost of what-I-might-have-been
stops thumping.

The ancestors of happiness have disappeared
a long time; they are hiding.
They appear as bats
and swirl like dark leaves
through my life,
they discuss the tribe's mistakes.

I believe in the goats that graze my neighbor's yard
and in Picasso's bronze goat standing in the museum
with seven cars, Ford Taurii, that hang from the lobby ceiling.
A Taurus was my first new car. When it was old,
my daughter drove it to college in Minnesota
where its belly rusted out from road salt.

I believe we inhabit cars the way we own our bodies—
precise, disheveled, picky, relaxed. And those trusted shells
carry us from the hospital, at birth, to the graveyard.

It's a mirage,
this passing down of caravan trails,
camels linked to each other,
so far between watering holes!

When I die, where to put my ashes?
My friend flies to her old town
to gather at her first husband's grave;

thirty years since he died. Now,
happily married, she still talks to John
on his death day. And so what?
Didn't I talk to those skulls in Cambodia, all piled
high behind glass cases? And shouldn't we pay
homage to those long passed? And what do we learn
at The Killing Fields, Dachau, the Sudan, Rwanda;
all the borders that scream *mine, mine mine?*

So many voices;
so many chants. It's hard
to hear the waterfall of faith.
It's hard to collect
the pebbles of belief.

It's the way ghosts live,
smoke and ashes,
this constant penance,
always asking advice.

But sometimes in the sand,
I find their tracks—
faint hieroglyphs,
marking the way.

Burning the Records

We brought the briquettes,
we brought the matches,
we brought the fuel:
fifteen years of tax returns,
cancelled checks, receipts.

Late October, we drove with
our big white dog
into the deserted park at sunset,
told the ranger, *Barbecue!*

And we found the biggest
group-shelter grill, on the edge
of a cold river, perfect
for the blazing.

As hills turned black
and the sun set over water
our fire grew hotter.
We spread the coals,
flames licking our sleeves
as we rearranged the pyre.

We fed the flames:
'93, '95, 2002—files, 1040's,
tax receipts—so many years
up in smoke, so much work
and money, dispensed, spent,
recorded, burned.

And the years,
like cancelled checks:
first a fist of pages,
fanning into leaves,
then curling into black ash;
until all that's left: burning
embers that climb
the night
sky.

The Café Is a Chapel for Sunlight

I have kept baby raccoons in my pockets for years.
They nuzzle my hips when I walk,
love the crumbs I drop when eating
croissants every morning in this cafe by the river.
I hear their little paws click.

Once I smelled smoke.
But saw nothing.
Maybe I smelled the ghost of smoke,
like I know Dorothy, my dead mother, is here,
in this cafe, along the river.

I don't have raccoons in my pocket.
I always wanted to, as a kid.
Now I'm in my fifty-sixth year.
Because I eat my vegetables I grow old.

The women at the weight-loss clinic keep
 talking about "saving their points"
 for the birthday party, but I'm saving my vegetables.
The green tomato of love; that's what got me here.
And the empty nest is what leaves me here.

The empty nest, a whir of promise—no interruptions! no birds!
They've all been eaten by the raccoons.
No, maybe the baby birds flew away.
Maybe they fell out of the nest. You'll never know.

And you won't know if this mother misses her children
or rejoices in their absence. All you'll know
is what will happen: she'll move out
in the world alive and green, a woman
past ripening, but with the fire of raccoons

in her pockets. Little gestures of hope
that wash their hands of the past.
Ce n'est pas rien. Ce n'est pas rien, they murmur.
And all the fountains with their waters of youth

will fold up their concrete dishes like flowers
in the evening and what will be left is the desert:
rabbitbrush, bitterbrush, Russian thistle,
which is not to say it won't bloom.

Four months after surgery

the woman with her husband's kidney
took me kayaking on the Columbia.
We paddled upriver against
the swift current trying to accomplish
one goal. And finally there,
at the old landing named, "ferry,"
—for a thing long gone—
we let ourselves drift back.

Our struggle had brought us
only this: warm sun,
cool water, and two boats
paused just long enough
to let the woman rescue a wasp
struggling with wet wings
on the surface of the water
in the middle of a wide river
with an island that presented
two young deer and,
all afternoon, a flock
of geese gathering
for flight.

About the Friend
—for D.

The cancer had spread to her bones.
She tried to imagine spring, lying in grass.
She did not want to lie down on the stone
heart of winter—as if she knew even angels
have wings that freeze. And how the shunt itched
but she needed it, the tubes connecting
her to drugs for chemo and pain
as if she were a fetus and this box she carried,
over her shoulder like a purse, was God.
And if it was, He had no mouth, was only a shadow
of something bigger—a taste on her tongue like iron
filings or anesthetic, the one they gave
her during her birth, the one that numbed
her all her life to the secrets
she was just learning: that every evening
could be anyone's last, and this world
was a swamp, night herons
stalking the shallows.

The Friend Speaks

Forget the extraordinary, I'm dying. Forget the trips to Costa Rica, the secret islands, the strange blue-green parrot I found in the pet store that reminds me of the Amazon and the trip I took at twenty-four to study indigenous people. Thirty-two and dying and all I want is to see a flock of starlings flip itself inside out, the snow frozen on the February sidewalk; how the sun finally appears after a week of gray.

I want to see the eyelash of desire, here in my own bed, with my own man, the slippers I slide my feet into each morning—to shuffle warm feet across a cold floor. The forming of words in my mouth, how even simple words— *yes, here, life, now*—mean more than any monks' manuscript hidden in a tower that I find on a trip to France. The tower is waiting for this exceptional tourist to climb the stairs and look into the glass case because it's next summer and I've survived another year.

Red Shrine under Madrona Tree

(on July 20th, a group of women hang a scarlet wedding sari in a tree, create a shrine to loss)

These red fields are not blood
but they could be.
And the red dime,
a coin minted in the country of grief

where pink saris
hang from trees
and the wind whispers
the names of colors:

fuchsia, red, pink,
all the flesh tones of our lives—
my red-lipsticked mother,
her pink nails,

how she wanted them painted
that last week in the hospital,
how the aides insisted:
all color removed.

As my memory of her is removed,
"a person I loved,"
that part's easy, the rest fades.

But outside at this makeshift shrine
she comes alive
in the folds of the windblown sari
we hang from the tree,

in the red shoes
and pink delphinium,
and the red notebook
with the red-tongued Kali
on the cover, dancing
atop Shiva, a god who sings,
a god who keens.

Two Poems from Camp

—written while serving as Resident Poet at N-Sid-Sen Camp for high school youth on the shores of Lake Coeur d'Alene

I. The First Night

This is the year of paved roads
—no tar and pebbles to distract us.
Last evening, a smooth drive into camp,
moonroof open, radio playing Lennon's *Imagine*
to the trees and sky.

This will be a year of music:
dancers in the pavilion,
guitars pulled straight from the fire.

A year of young men and women,
forty-one to forty-five;
finally, the numbers almost even!

And don't forget the Bear,
his secret watch from
the rendezvous bush.

Make this a year of new friends,
the shy and loud—
each seeking to be known
as a unique point of light
in our N-Sid-Sen sky.

And make this a year of immersion:
water in the lake, rain from on high.
Last night we swam
that lake and I saw how black
the world can be, beyond
a small flashlight on the dock—
How lonely!—if not for friends,
their voices calling
back and forth
across dark waters.

II. The Last Morning

We've spent a week
forgetting our other selves—
no cell phones ringing our brains,
no email knocking at cyber doors.

This place. The sounds: woodpeckers
and sparrows, even screaming pterodactyls.

We can bring it home in photo and word,
but only the heart can remember
our singing out over the lake,
or night music wrapping around us on the porch.

We can pretend we understand peace,
do skits on delivering babies,
even make a meadow into a theater—incredible!
But we can't pretend each other.

How your lives entwined into my own
this week and travelers from Angola
to Teko wove a basket of community.

An eye for an eye is one kind of life,
but I say for seven days you've bathed
in holy water, torched your old identity
in the fire. Return to your other world
reconciled, free; and wear
this week's beauty like a scar.

Bathing Cyrus

With the other dogs it was a wrestling
match but this one led himself over
the edge of the tub into the warm
water. "Is he ill?" I wondered
then remembered his lineage:
show dogs, and all that grooming
in his genes. I removed the red collar—
his only clothes—and with care spilled
water down the white back and legs, tilting
his tranquil face towards the light. Washing
him I remembered my long-grown babies,
the pleasures of bath time. And the dog
stood there, taking it all in, the soaping
and rinsing, Mahler on the radio,
my fingers rubbing his ears,
my lips kissing the top of his wet
muzzle, the dirt swirling down
the drain, and all the while I'm crooning
good dog, good dog, good dog.

Vacation Maui

It's the holiday mask we wear
the iridescent curl of lips,
slightly parted as if lost clothing
and empty gas tanks don't matter,
we're on vacation!

It's not that we can't enjoy a luxury trip
—shuttered windows and bare arms.
We remember those feelings,
but it's ruined by the company towns:
smoke rising from fields burning our eyes.

After a week we look past
the sugar factories—their history
the same as all factories—finally relax,
ease our bodies into water,

fin and float our way across coral reefs
with barely a scratch, breathe
through a plastic tube
that ties us to a world we ignore,
the world the *nunu* fish know nothing about.

One day we take a boat to an underwater volcano
—hundreds of tourists thrashing
the water. Other boats feed the fish;
not ours, we're the Whale Foundation,
ecologically smart.
                          After the frenzy settles,
the water is transparent, the world suddenly
more than its surface. We swim, the family
together, apart, for hours.

When the boat goes to leave,
one tourist missing—we name her
The Lost Elizabeth. Everyone searches, the water
so clear we know she hasn't drowned.
Finally, they call over speakers and she waves
from the boat next door, thought it looked "different."

She laughs, her husband embarrassed at holding up the tour.
It's like that sometimes—the body gravitating
towards a place it doesn't recognize
nor belong, yet pretends is home.

At the next stop we swim near Turtle Arches,
see the world outside from the water below.
I count white-spotted puffins, motion my daughters
towards goatfish that hover above coral, sway
with underwater swells. We dive lower
and see the urchins, once harvested by missionaries
then dried for writing—*slate pencils*.

Suddenly we spot the sea turtles,
give them space, tread backwards
as each one paddles up for air,
as if planned for a "photo op."

And we take turns swimming past them,
pose for the underwater camera,
suck in our bellies for the world
we'll bring this home to.

Still Awake at 2 AM, Quoting Whitman

The dog licks his crotch again,
trots to the toilet for a drink.

Urge and urge and urge

You try not to turn, roll, toss, cough,
    wake your husband, sleeping.

Think of your body as cement: no thoughts.

Think of the penguins with limited mobility—
        best option: live in Ushuaia.

Remember the last time you made love, the last time
        you didn't.

He rises now and leaves you for the guest
        room—every insomniac's rival.

It's better this way, soon his side
        of the bed will be cool; you'll go there.

Hurrah for positive science.

You imagine your white blood cells:
little sleeping bichons,
red cells: trotting ponies.
But what about the platelets?

The Lord is lonely, that's why he wants you awake.

I find letters from God dropped in the street.

"You will be transformed, a new leaf,"

saith the Lord, "tomorrow night you sleep."

Thai Bus Trip

How did we get stuck?
I thought we had a plan;
it was about new beginnings.
Have you ever been on a bus tour that
has no destination because the final stop
is the international airport,
closed by protests
for over a week?

It turns a trip into a wild playground,
with fourteen other passengers.
Hank always trespassing on my mind,
saying, "I bet you want a drink,"
when, really, he was the one who bought
three cheap beers every night,
snuck them into the restaurant
in a 1-liter water bottle. It looked
like a 24-hour urine sample.

"Never again," I said
to my husband who was escaping
the charms of Lily, a sixty-four-
year-old widow with stiff red hair,
cakes of makeup, and a tiptoe walk;
she was always complaining.

Everyone avoided her—
the scapegoat;
but I figured she voiced
our feelings:
tired and cranky.

It didn't matter,
Lily, who never got off
the bus and was afraid of lice,
basically told everyone,

"Greet yourself." Which was her way
of saying "Fuck off!"

II.

Remember those dreams
you took for granted?

You scheduled this exotic trip because
your future may be clouded. (You
had gone to a big-city doc just in case
you ever needed one—he orders routine
blood work: *Surprise! Leukemia!*
No treatment yet, wait and see.)

Sometimes it's better not to know.
What can you do? Drink bottled
water? Eat fillet of sole?
Leave on a trip where you travel
like Hannibal, riding an elephant
only this one also paints—self-portraits
where she's standing
on hind legs shooting
baskets with her trunk.
This is true, you can buy
the painting for $50.00.

The trainer claims the elephant
loves art; he sleeps by her side every night.
Perhaps that part is also true,
just like this bus ride
wheeling though Thailand
while the government's shut down:
yellow shirts vs. red shirts.
Our guide, Anu, says, "Thailand
peaceful country. You must
complete the tour."

Bursts of white pass—orchids,
Buddhist nuns—white chunks of sound
from the tour guide that reach me
in the back of the bus.
I am tired.
I wish I had fireplugs

to put in my ears.
I wish I had an unhurried
spin of days instead of one temple,
one monument, one elephant-
river-ride after another.

Everyone's afraid we'll be here
for a month riding
this bus with Buzz,
Walt, Charlene, and our own Liz
who brings plastic wrap
to snatch biscuits from breakfast.

My skin is aging. I buy Retin A, cheap,
without a prescription, at a pharmacy;
I tell all the women. Soon we
pile off the bus and load up.

At least if we're stuck here forever
we'll end up looking
like fine young beauties.

After the woman left Orvieto

it all went fine, even though they were driving
without insurance. She started drinking
wine again. She gave up on mad cow,
mucca pazzia, and ordered *cinghiale*
every night. Her old thoughts were packed
in the suitcase lost at the airport,
so her conclusions were gone,
along with the black skirt
and the golden slippers,
along with the silk robe
and its garden of flowers,

The suitcase went to Belgium
but she, she went to Umbria.
She went to see the Fra Lippo Lippi
in the Duomo in Spoleto. She went to sip
cappuccino, let the feeling of morning
come down her veins. She read
the strange maps with a facile tongue,
tasted her husband's mouth and found
herself fluent in new ways.

Maybe this was good.
They didn't wreck the car, a Fiat,
and they didn't lose the suitcase forever.
About mad cow, it's too early to say.

The day the plein air painting

class met it was hot,
exuberant, after months
of gray. I turned left
at the *Jesus is Lord* sign
and met six women,
at the Jesus is Lord Beach.

Vermilion, ochre, cerulean blue,
the colors were all out that day,
and we learned to create
the palest wash, search the horizon
for light and shadow.

We painted on the muddy banks
of Chimacum Creek, while heron
kept watch and eagles circled.
We worked all afternoon
until the tide filled the creek
to overflowing.

Then we stripped off our clothes
and entered the water—
left the shadows of the trees
to become the light
in our very own landscape.

The Buddha says

to hold both opposites—joy
and pain. Live in this acceptance
as if our minds were doing parlor
games when they fall in love and hate,
as if the sly tricks of the old fox
don't matter. Here, the woman
behind the register counts
change as if the 16 cents mattered. Money
changing hands is nothing these days—
it's electronic transfers that count.

And what else counts? We believe
we saw penguins in Puerto Monte, Chile—
Patagonia—but David and Susie swore,
that when they were there, they saw fields
of flamingos. Who's right? Maybe no one—
maybe Buddha would say it's an illusion.

Last week, when I asked the monk
about illusions, he was distracted;
perhaps it was the audience of a thousand
and he, on the stage about to speak,
sitting in a leather club chair
from Restoration Hardware.

My friend, also at the conference,
is a Quaker; won't buy anything
from China—"factories are too primitive—
pollution, cheap labor," she says.

Cheap labor, that's what I felt
like as a young mother, doing physical
work from dawn to midnight,
till I'd finally pour a glass of cabernet
and retire to a notebook and a blank page.

A blank page—and what have I written
across all these years of joy and suffering?
A crow, a locket, an amulet.

IV

Magellan's Right Turn

after seeing a painting, *Magellan's Right Turn,*
in oil and beeswax by Jeane Myers
                    —for S.

This painting hangs in a show
of happy events: *Blue Orb, Green*
Energy, Skagit Valley on Mesh.

All have singing colors except for *Magellan's Right Turn,*
which is faded black, white, and sepia; burnt umber,
sienna, and Payne's gray washed down the center,
of what? A femur? A coffin? There is no flesh
in this painting; it hangs,
skeletal, on the wall.

It's true, this morning my yoga teacher
told us we would rise from corpse
pose, just as they say Jesus rose,
but no body is rising from this painting.
Its bones are picked clean,
washed with tears till they shine,
luminous, in the spotlight of this gallery.

Miles away my friend struggles,
fights for her life,
or fights against her death.
It's hard to say which
she will choose at what moment
after years of metastatic cancer.

Five years ago she told me,
"It's in the bones,"
now visions from those years:
morning walks along her desert river
(Canada geese rising), a return
to Australia's Blue Mountains
(scent of eucalyptus from her childhood),
her husband's steady hands as he ferries
her to treatments in Seattle

(blizzard in the winter mountains).
These images, along with the needles,
are scratched in her memory
as the surface of this painting,
covered with beeswax,
is etched with lines, the way her face
has become lined with our grief
and her own grief, as we sail
this uncharted ocean.

Forgetting the Word for Weep

This is the day your aunt lets you kiss her twice,
once when you say hello and she cries, calls
you by her sister's name, and once when you leave,
her cheek soft as the childhood mare you lost
to the all-night colic.

And this is the day you return to your father's,
trying to say good-bye, your plane about to leave,
and he wants to show you pictures,
slides of childhood—thirty carousels, thirty slides each—
you saw them all yesterday, your dead mother with you
as a child, and her smile, almost happy,
as she poses, always, in tight sweaters, a figure
she would envy from the grave.

And this is the day you will return home to your husband;
but first, you ride the plane, just behind a man
and his young family who are separated
by the aisle. He is talking too loud
to his small daughter about people
who use blow-up dummies to sneak
rides in car pool lanes.

Now he is doing a crossword with his wife,
four seats away. They are calling back and forth
for a four-letter word that means shedding tears;
you think of cry but it is only three and the woman minister
next to you is arguing with seat 3C about Jesus as a feminist
and you want to tell them all to shut up, your father is dying
and your aunt has Alzheimer's, and you're leaving,
grateful, guilty, trying to find words to fill in the spaces,
each and every box.

The Geri-Psych Ward

We were told to bring nothing
sharp, no framed pictures, scissors,
nail files, needles,
nothing with cords or coils,
like electric razors,
never any rope,
but bring small things to amuse:
cards, simple puzzles.
Still my eighty-five-year-old father
manages to slip a pocket knife
into the ward, force
the rules like water seeking
its own level or the patients
that gather before the light
of the nurses' station,
some half-dressed in gowns
and urine-soaked diapers,
hair white or snow-rooted.
They spend their days in groups,
finger small tiles in occupational therapy,
hammer nails the aides carefully count.
Late afternoon, they slouch
against each other on day couches,
lean into their night.

The woman could not forget

her father down twenty minutes of back
roads, in the nursing home, the wind
always blowing her like a sailboat
as she crossed the asphalt parking lot,
propelled in her family's demise.

The woman could not forget sailing with him
at the lake, the white caps choppy
with agitation some cool mornings;
she could not remember the calm
days of childhood, though like water
she knew they were there below
the surface and, with an anchor,
could be reached.
But she didn't want to go there.

Her head ached from
all the effort. Her heart ached
from all the longing. It was dangerous
to remember the good times,
for who would hold her
and bless her as she failed,
once more, with her father?

And this was his final triumph:
how each day he sank
softly and smoothly out of reach
into the silky fathoms of his death.

When it happened

there was a lifting
as the world rises after rain,
as the shaved head of the monk lifts
after prayer, but this was a lifting not of angels
winged to paradise, but hearts like rock tied by rope
to an ancient machine that was cranked tighter and tighter
then suddenly let go
and the rock and rope unravel
in a weighted loosening.

And I walked to the sink, drank
a plastic cup of water, returned to the scaffold
of his bed and stared, aslant.
I could not look death
straight on.

When it happened there was a lifting,
the days and weeks and years rushing
out the window, the small mirror over the sink
looking back at me, its face mouthing the o's,
of "it's over, it's over," and the pause
between that final last breath,
which had happened again and again
for hours, and the true one,
that pause which now would last forever
and go from lifting and opening to gathering
weight, that pause finally ended
and slowly the lifting began to loosen,
the arms that had been open
folded across the body, the mouth
that exhaled its last, closed, a rolled towel
under the chin. The nurses have been called,
now, and they are doing that at which they excel,
being quietly busy, and when it happened
there was a lifting, but now the machinery
of the world begins once more, and I
will pick up the weight of this death
and carry it with me long after
his body returns to the earth.

Also the Rising

It was easy, then, to stay on the surface.
Summer, all the fountains bubbling,
all the white pelicans floating on the river—
wingspans so wide they frightened the dog.
No thoughts of death, its sunny weather,
no thoughts of minutes passing, the days
all scented with almonds, not grief.

There are those who remark
it must be hard to lose your last parent.
I do not tell them it's a relief
to have the burdens of childhood lifted
dripping from my shoulders, a yoke of buckets
I was tired of hauling. And yes,
it's also sad, different from the pain
I carried when my mother died.
This is more complex than the simplicity
of his ghost hovering. I am stranded
on an island formed by two rivers,
the good father and the bad father,
and I can see at the far end
they come together like fused bone,
like the arms of a jacket come together
to cover the chest and it becomes one
garment you must wear to keep

you warm as you enter cold storage
and your feet cross the sawdust-covered
floor and you search the rows of ice blocks
looking for what you put there years ago—
your heart—which you must now carry outside
to sunlight where it will melt,
water the ground.

Three Poems with Light

I.

The woman thought there was never enough light,
even when she pulled back the sheer
curtains and painted all rooms white.
She moaned over any shadow,
any darkness. She wanted a house like a car
—windows on all sides—and she policed
her entire family, even from a distance.
"Are your shades open, are you turned
south, your face radiant and welcoming
to everyone who passes?" It was rapture,
this idea of sun, and should rain return
to mock her she would claim
the weather was a momentary mistake,
her world was always meant to shine.

II.

The heart says *escape without a trace*
and that's the mystery
of his leaving, how the pattern
of his death pulled
everything at the seams
even though she knew it was coming.
Even though he was the last,
his body rising
and falling beneath
the white sheets, his rattled
whispers of breath, nothing
but common. A year later
she can still remember the sun
outside his window and how,
after hours at his side,
she had to walk there,
in the light, if only for ten minutes.

And she knew that while she was walking
he would leave for good,

such was the bond between the father
and the daughter he always abandoned.

III.

It was now that part of her life
—in the shadows—
and how could this abysmal
longing be true?
Even the snapdragons
held sorrow.

Let the air circulate
on all dark things: fog, mist,
the forgetfulness of memory.
Add a tincture to the gray
sky and clear away the rain.
It's a good life and good faith
is what you had to take tomorrow
on; multiple kisses, multiple bruises.
It's all the same tunnel called life
and you're sucked in,
you have to let go,
and meanwhile
the angels lean back,
fan their wings.

This Story, This Happiness
—for Sharon

Do not paint the stories of your people,
paint the dream of the stories of your people.—Chagall

The story could be the cancer
metastasized to her bones,
the words, its manifestation in blood
counts. "Bone-mets," she told
me over green tea, "the cells are wily;
one chemo works, then, suddenly
you have to switch." But she's not changing
this time. She's going, with her sister,
to England on the *Queen Mary,*
then meeting her husband in Paris.

Six months ago, when she planned this voyage,
I worried she wouldn't make it.
Just before she left she called and said,
"My tumor markers spiked.
I'm ignoring it till I return."

On my wall, a photo of a frozen
waterfall. Each branch outlined
with veins of snow, every boulder
covered in sheets of white. Icicles
on the bridge etch the atmosphere
with their silence.
The rush of water over rock,
held in midair.

Suspended animation, this autumn journey
she takes across the Atlantic; wrapped
in down, sipping cappuccino,
watching the sea.

Soon she'll return
and continue treatment,
but for now she's frozen
in the beauty of time,
without alchemy, without regret.

Where We Come From

I come from the truth hidden behind
Mother's breastbone and the concrete
hearts of all the distant fathers.

The day I was almost struck
by lightning all I had to show
for it was singed tennis shoes.

We were living in Boulder
then, sky sparked with storm clouds,
winds so strong they'd swirl the water
in the upstairs toilet.

When we left Boulder for California,
I told my children, "Okay, so you're
sick of moving, but imagine
you're a pioneer, or a migrating dolphin."

That held them for an hour, at most;
but we are what we are, and children
are hallelujah fruit pies—
happy and sticky and you're stained
with their love forever.

"If I were a whimbrel I'd live
near the sea." "So what!" my husband
replied. "You're a person and we live
in the desert." This was later,
after we'd left California and returned
to the Eastern Washington landscape.
He was reluctant to hear I wanted to move, again.

When you spend your childhood waiting
for the moving van, you never learn
to relax. The jealous volcano of wanting
something new spills out onto the late-summer
lawn and before you know it you're sorting
dishes, collecting raffia for the packing crate.
Even now I remember Alaska; that summer

I was ten and we lived near the mudflats
of Cook Inlet. How I'd walk the railroad tracks
and when I came to the bridge I'd stop,
look ahead, behind, then run across holding
my breath, glancing down, down, down
through the spaces between the ties.

'Where were my parents?' I wonder,
to let me cross a railroad bridge by myself
and sometimes with Keno, my dog,
in my arms…

And when I tell this to my friend, Linda,
she wonders where her parents
were to let her climb into a rowboat
with the neighbor boy, both about twelve,
and row out onto Useless Bay,
water so cold hypothermia
hits in fifteen minutes and, besides,
they didn't have life preservers—

Mostly none of us had life jackets
back then—and still, we survived.

And isn't that how we all survive:
day by day?

                    Until we find ourselves
in Rio careening around the corner
in a taxi driven by Camello, the crazy driver,
—they're all crazy!—
boulevards five lanes wide,
no lines, everyone weaving
and darting in an endless stream,
like sperm that finally made
their way to our mother's nest,
that place we all come from.

Where do they go

all those exhaled breaths?
They come in new, then leave
like ancient writings—
these people lived, died,
hunted gazelle, collected grain.
The breaths that leave
tell that kind of story.
And when the air is chilled,
we can watch their parting.

My husband measures noise
from stars. A globe of the world
encased in a clear sphere
sits on his desk. The names
of constellations are written
there: *Cassiopeia,*
Lacerta, Cygnus, the swan.
You can spin the globe
to match the seasons or twirl
it in a timeless haze.

We all know heaven
doesn't enclose the world
like his plastic sphere,
that our breaths ring
out far beyond the farthest
sky; they circle there,
lost and hopeful, ahead
and before time, saying,
"I'm from Jim," and sometimes,
"It was hard"; mingling
together in a quiet mist—
beyond the moon, beyond the sun,
beyond gleaming, noisy stars.

The Stones and the Weather

This is the town with antique stores
and cobblestones, with water
lapping its tongue on both sides,
ghosts in old parade grounds,
a rusted car on every block.

Net tenders lived here, officers
and their wives, like my mother-in-law
who lived in the salmon-colored Henry
House, now a jewel of historic homes,
on tour bright spring mornings.

I have come here to live,
to understand my time as a mannequin
in the window of wifehood,
to forgive the pose I struck—
always a smile for the photographer
and one eye on the children
who never played in the street.

I have come here from the shrub steppe
of middle age, when everyone
above me on the generational ladder
was stepping off and they asked me for
small sheets of paper—to make lists.

Father, in his dementia,
wanted me to write down the name
of each of his dead siblings: Don,
Ed, Mildred, Lee, and Bob—
his name. One by one he had me cross
them out—*all gone!*
except for himself, the last.

He spoke no words, just moved his fingers
across the names;
had me follow with the pencil.

He took the list, folded it once,

placed it in his pocket.
He carried it around all day,
called it his *"obits list,"* patted
his side. At night he had the aide
place it on the nightstand near his bed.

Now he's gone and I've come here
from that dusty town that bloomed
like the mushroom cloud it helped create.

I am not the mannequin in the store
window anymore, nor am I the daughter
creating lists. I am sea kelp drifting
the Strait of Juan de Fuca—
the ghost that rattles inside Fort bunkers,
the moss that weeps in the old-growth
forest. I am the Point Wilson lighthouse,
sending its beacon, *It's me. It's me.*
I am the orange sun rising
above Mt. Baker, the watcher.

All the Birds Awake

It had been a year since his wife died and now her brother was sitting on our woman's deck, fountain bubbling in the background.

The brother leaned forward, answered the woman's questions, *how was he, what's happening*— all predictable—but the woman thought her brother had changed; he looked tired. Was it weight loss to save his ticking heart, or was it grief that had painted his face with new lines?

Fruit flies hovered in the kitchen, a jet liner was crashing in the Atlantic, and the chocolate pearl the woman had purchased from a street vendor in Majorca was about to fall out of its setting.

Her sister-in-law had left her setting—gracious house with view of San Francisco Bay—and now she rested in an urn. Since then our woman has become obsessed with death. How do people make it to eighty? she wondered. She felt like Hannibal crossing the Alps in winter—so many obstacles and only seven elephants, a few wishes, one life.

Predators were killing cats right and left; only last month her neighbors saw their Miss Ditz dangle in the jaws of an early-morning coyote. They went into a deep depression.

But our woman was on her deck talking about the roofs in Dubrovnik— how that jeweled city was bombed in the nineties, how red tile roofs have been restored. The woman remembers mosaics she'd seen there in the museum.

A few days ago, a pop icon died. The world was waiting for his funeral. Just yesterday she was able to clean the bird shit from her windshield while still driving—automatic wipers!

Water always made her happy, the aqua Adriatic on a recent cruise, the community pool where she'd bobbed like a cork, her late evening soaks in the tub reading the morning news.

Breakfast dishes lay on the garden table. She tried to skewer the memory of this time: sun, her sweet brother, all the birds awake and singing; flags being raised for the Fourth; the rest of her family coming to visit. Life was like that fourteen-headed fountain in Dubrovnik; drink from all the faucets, the world brings you luck.

Ketchikan

Tonight, dinner in an old Seattle hotel,
dark interiors, velvet drapes, real fire in this
lounge called *hunt club*, and suddenly
we're our long-dead parents, drinking
scotch, manhattans, ordering appetizers
as if there's no final bill.

Yesterday we said good-bye
to a friend—this was on the dry
side of the mountains, all russian thistle,
bitterbrush, outside the windows
where her service was held.

Someone read that poem about wild
geese, about letting your body
love what it loves, and I thought
of her return to Australia's Blue Mountains,
childhood home, where she swam
under waterfalls, watched Rosella parrots
color blue-leafed eucalyptus trees,

and like the geese who did
a fly-by during the Service,
the next day we migrate
to our new home—cross the Pass
just cleared from a blizzard, meet
old friends in this dim restaurant.

We are drinking merlot now, grown
and aged in the Horse Heaven Hills,
and we toast the one just gone,
and ourselves, who remain,

and while we're at it we plan
a trip to Ketchikan this August—
a long drive, but who cares?

Our lives are swirling forward,
one course after another,
the salmon will be running—
silvers flashing the late summer air.

Alchemy

Pushing on through the scrim of days
it seemed there was a mountain
outside her congenial life: the storms
that came down, and the rain.
Once she saw a shooting star.
They were in the desert beside the Place
of Coyotes where they were camping
in a Volkswagen bus the size of a glove
box. A glove box, one of those boxes
her physicist husband used to handle
radioactive materials.

When they first married
he would come home from work all flushed
and eager like the wind. He'd come home
to his young wife and babies
and it seemed to her he had a radiance
about him as if nuclear particles
of joy had attached themselves
to his fleece, as if their marriage
wasn't a mistake and he
wasn't afraid to spend fifty
more years with this woman
who seemed almost a tree,
madrona, with all its
layers that kept revealing his dreams.
Like the sand tray therapy she did
in her work. Children
would come to her office,
rearrange Mother, Father, Baby,
in the sand, maybe add a dog.
Then, surely, trouble: some ghostly figure
would appear, interrupt their lives on the dunes.

Their life on the dune of early
marriage was a thick glass vase—
Waterford or Baccarat—about to shatter.
But life brought so many terrors and pleasures
that the hairline cracks fused,

the fractures never split.
It was cold sometimes, and often there
was thin ice to cross,
but they always ended up together—
thirty-four years of this mystery,
a midden filled with fragments
and shards of pottery jars,
a hillock that would stand
like an ancient burial ground,
like the ring he bought her
for 25 bucks that lasted years.
And the gem, not really a ruby,
merely sparkly glass, never
lost its color, like this marriage
that turns water into wine.

Anniversary: Icicle Creek

All night the river made its water-sound,
the low rustle over rocks like radio
static. All night the woman slept
deep in the bed with her husband.
Thirty years earlier they stayed
in another cabin near another river
and last night they proclaimed:
 "Neither one of us has changed!"

It's true, they've been blessed,
two daughters, now grown. No cancers
taking her breasts, his testicles. "A miracle
to start old age intact!" he said, and she smiled
in spite of the wounds they wore, the scars;
how love had brought them here in some insistent
way like the river that all night
refuses to slow down,
even while they sleep.

How were we to know

it might have been the final time?
The last had been a week earlier
and then we got the news:
prostate cancer, surgery needed
right away. We could have gone
home, jumped into bed,
but we were shocked,
stunned, and the next day,
facing death, he turned away.

How were we to know
it could be different?
No more ease and glide,
the reckless rising,
our bodies working their riffs
in constant variations.

And how many times does one remember
exactly? The time in that room
paneled with smoky mirrors,
outside under backcountry stars,

all the exquisite journeys
at the edge of unraveling—
visual flashes of our bedrooms—
intricate designs on fading paper,
some *thing,* often, about candles
or the light, music from endless players,
and ourselves, the played,

the mirroring blue of our eyes,
his body's rendering above/beneath me;
his pale skin, its star-shaped mole;
all the secret latching and unlocking
of our bodies together, one seamless
conversation. And this may be the last,

this time I take you into me,
try to memorize the exact shape
of your life, how effortlessly it fits
into mine, then slips away.

Because at the core
—for Bill

we are strong but think we are weak,
we need to consider our hearts as temple bells
ringing with the resonance of mountain villages
twelve-thousand feet high, no vertigo,
only breathlessness. Pretend we've returned
from Lhasa and the leaves as gold there
as yesterday, when we drove home from Seattle
on back roads by the shimmer of river, the shadows
playing with the light.

Autumn, then,
and you have just had a deep surgery
that brutalized your body.
Yes, we say, the tumor danced
in its formaldehyde jar and is gone!

Let me rub your wounds with oil.
Breathe in and in, no need to worry.
The past is a grain of rice. Who cares
what happened; you were asleep.

But we all know the body holds
that knife somewhere in its memory,
and your work now is to calm the cells.
Pick up windfall apples from this October
storm, carry them to the cellar in a basket
called hope. Gather all the random fruit
and late-afternoon light,
the day a candle flickering. . .

We're at a summer gathering—

warm night near the water—
and I'm wearing a zebra print
shirt because everyone at this Bar-Be
is retired and going to Botswana this spring,
except for my old roommate who is visiting

and probably thinking, "Thank
God I don't have money
to burn and won't be traveling
with these codgers and have to laugh
at their jokes."—which after two cocktails,
seem pretty funny.

I brought the cocktails,
a mix of cranberry,
seltzer, vodka, and lime.

I made a big deal
out of it—brought nothing
else—no salad with radicchio,
no crackers and paté, no homemade
blueberry pie; not even a relish tray.

But " I brought the drinks!"
I announced. Except when I went
to make them I discovered I'd left
the vodka home on the counter,
having mixed a little trial
for my friend which we promptly drank.
So I had to "borrow" the host's vodka.

It's like that sometimes; you attempt
a good deed and it goes to hell,
though we ended up fine—
a bunch of wildebeests
at the watering hole,
swishing our tails and nuzzling
each other—happy to be alive—
another day on the savannah.

In These Canyons

. . . to the Navajo. . .the passage of time is not important.
—National Park Service brochure, Canyon de Chelly

"Nobody does these road trips
anymore," I tell my husband.
"They're cruising the Marquesas,
kayaking the coast of Baja."

Still, the two of us are following
the old routes: U.S. 66, Arizona 264,
one road even called "the loneliest in America."

We're driving the Southwest—
Durango, Moab, Chinle.
We're listening to music;
today, a requiem.

Yesterday, the Navajo guide told us a story.
"We are in the Fourth World, the Glittering World,"
she said. And there *was* a glow—sunrise rinsing
the mesa in pink, and later, purple shadows
sliding down sandstone walls.

Always, Father Sky. His wide smile
looking down at our day's routine:
breakfast of cold cereal; pack the car; get in
and drive, the wheels grinding
our worries to sand. Where to stay the night?
Whether to stop beside the road and buy
the *yei be che* weaving from the grandmother.

One day we wander for hours
along a canyon ridge, stumble
into a silence we had almost forgotten.

We are together, this man and I
and we are traveling,
across a vast landscape,
growing smaller.

We are listening to music, stories,
and the canyons.
We are hiking—Mesa Verde,
Arches, Canyon de Chelly,
searching.

　　　　It's about heat,
sandstone, and petroglyphs;
red rock, pinnacles, and pictographs—
of horses, sheep, even domesticated dogs.
　　　　It's about cliff
dwellings: how the Ancient Ones
huddled together under a wall
of sheer rock—
a brief moment,
a pottery shard,
a glint of mica in the sand.

The Columbia: A Baptism 1975-2005

—upon seeing a painting of baptism, *The Beauty of Chance*, by Perry
Woodfin

I.

They come together in water,
saved by the mud of religion,
each nose and head held
by a man who speaks for God.

II.

Hannah kept her baby's ashes
in a box in the closet,
never cried, until one day
she sat down beside the river,
began sketching the trees.

III.

Benches with brass plaques
line the path beside the river.
Karen has her own bench now—
sixteen, killed by a reckless driver.

IV.

In the painting, people
wear their Sunday best
to be rinsed in the river.

V.

One summer the teens ask
for baptism in the river,
a lark for our liberal church.
Sandra plays her guitar.
Steve performs the submersion.

Amelia wears a white dress;
her dog follows into the water, barking.

VI.

We walked every morning
beside the river.
Just west of Swimmer's Beach,
a new linden tree;
Sharon's there now.

VII.

The watercolor of baptism
reveals several preachers,
several saved. The painting,
mostly black and white, turns
all the details gray.

VIII.

On the shore: two boulders
with brass letters in Vietnamese;
one rock for each girl who decides,
one evening, to swim to the island,
not far; they never make it.

IX.

At our place beside the Columbia:
upstream, a nuclear waste dump;
downstream, a chemical weapons depot;
across from where we lived, an island
alive with white pelicans.

X.

Before moving, I water-ski
one last time. At dusk
we build a fire.
Just before moonrise,
the water turns black.

About The Author

Gayle Kaune has been published widely in literary magazines including *Poet and Critic, Willow Springs, Crab Creek Review, Seattle Review, Milkweed Editions, South Florida Poetry Review,* and *Centennial Review.* She has won several Washington Poets Awards, a Ben Hur Lampmann Award, and has been nominated for a Pushcart Prize. Her first book, *Still Life in the Physical World,* was published by Blue Begonia Press. She also has two chapbooks: *N'Sid-Sen-Star* and *Concentric Circles,* which won the Flume Press Award.

She graduated from Occidental College and has an MA from Stanford University and an MSW from Walla Walla University. She has worked as a junior high and high school teacher as well as a psychotherapist. She is a licensed clinical social worker. A co-founder of the Rattlesnake Mountain Writers' Workshop, she is now on the Centrum Writers' Conference Advisory Board.

After spending more than twenty-five years in the Eastern Washington desert and raising two daughters there, she moved, with her husband and their big white dog, to Port Townsend, Washington, where they live alongside an old-growth forest. She has four lively grandchildren.

THE TEBOT BACH MISSION

The mission of Tebot Bach is to strengthen community, to promote literacy, to broaden the audience for poetry by community outreach programs and publishing, and to demonstrate the power of poetry to transform life experiences through readings, workshops and publications.

THE TEBOT BACH PROGRAMS

1. A poetry reading and writing workshop series for venues which serve marginalized populations such as homeless shelters, battered women's and men's shelters, nursing homes, senior citizen daycare centers, Veterans organizations, hospitals, AIDS hospices, and correctional facilities, and for schools K-College. Participating poets include: John Balaban, M.I. Liebler, Patricia Smith, Dorianne Laux, Laurence Lieberman, Richard Jones, Arthur Sze and Carol Moldaw.

2. A poetry reading and writing workshop series for the community Southern California at large. The workshops feature local, national, and international teaching poets. Participating poets include: David St. John, Charles Webb, Wanda Coleman, Amy Gerstler, Patricia Smith, Holly Prado, Dorothy Barresi, W.D. Ehrhart, Tom Lux, Rebecca Seiferle, Suzanne Lummis, Michael Datcher, B.H. Fairchild, Cecilia Woloch, Chris Abani, Laurel Ann Bogen, Sam Hamill, David Lehman, and Mark Doty.

3. A publishing component in order to give local, national, and international poets a venue for publishing and distribution.

Grateful acknowledgement is given to Steve and Lera B. Smith, our donors, and to Golden West College in Huntington Beach, California, all of whom make our programs possible.

TEBOT BACH
HUNTINGTON BEACH • CALIFORNIA
WWW.TEBOTBACH.ORG